Predestined to Hell?

Why Would a God of Love Consign People to Hell FOREVER?

Kevin Madison

Copyright ©2021 Kevin Madison

All rights reserved. This book or any portion thereof may not be reproduced or used in any manner whatsoever without the express written permission of the publisher except for the use of brief quotations in a book review.

ISBN: 978-1-7377003-0-2 paperback
ISBN: 978-1-7377003-1-9 ebook

Cover design and publishing assistance by The Happy Self-Publisher
Published by Madison Christian Books, LLC

Kevin J. Madison
Founder: Treasure in Every Verse Ministry
Owner: Madison Christian Books, LLC
925 S. Lewis St. #255
New Iberia, LA 70560
Website: kevinjmadison.com
Email: tevm9328@gmail.com

To my wife, Cynthia Madison, who encouraged me to pursue my passion for studying the word of God, writing and publishing this book to the glory of the Most High God. I pray the Lord Jesus will continue to enable me to love you like the Father loves Israel, and He loves his bride, the Church.

Contents

Introduction vii

Part 1: Our Identity 1

    Chapter 1: Two Types of People 3

    Chapter 2: The Enemy of God 5

    Chapter 3: Is there really a hell? 9

    Chapter 4: Who is Jesus Christ? 21

Part 2: In Christ Alone by Faith Alone 25

    Chapter 1: Jesus Christ is God the Savior 27

    Chapter 2: Condemned? Why God? 33

    Chapter 3: There is Hope in Jesus and the Evidence of Saving Faith 47

Notes 53

About The Author 55

Introduction

Do you know anyone who has questions about whether they are traveling the road to heaven or hell?

Maybe you are searching for the answer to that question. Which road are you on?

Is the roadway filled with potholes?

Are the lanes uneven?

Are there street signs leading you in the right direction to your destination?

So many choices, so little time, which to choose?

Predestined to Hell? investigates the two roads, identifying the warning signs on the road to hell and confirming the street signs on the road to heaven.

Are you a Christian but struggle to witness and fully explain the gospel?

Then hand them this book. The path to salvation is clearly presented. Keep a copy handy to help you explain the gospel the next time the Holy Spirit prompts you to witness, while building up your most holy faith.

PART 1

OUR IDENTITY

CHAPTER 1

Two Types of People

The Lord has chosen and called out a remnant from among the peoples of the world, which includes both Jews and Gentiles (non-Jewish). These called out people are better known as the Church, the body of Christ. *"...And He (God the Father) put all things under His (Jesus) feet and gave Him (Jesus) to be head over all things to the church [22]..., [23]which is His body, the fullness of Him who fills all in all."* **Eph. 1:22-23**

Another name for the true Church is believers, and another name for earth dwellers (those who have no concern for anything except that which resides here on earth and not in heaven) is unbelievers. We should define both.

Believers—those who have confessed to God that they are lost sinners and have received Christ as Lord and Savior. All their sins, past, present, and future, have been transferred from their account onto Jesus' upon the cross and three (3) days in the grave. The proof that God has accepted Christ's substitutionary sacrifice is the bodily resurrection of His Son, Jesus, from the grave and seating him upon the throne in heaven, thereby giving Jesus all authority in heaven and earth. God treated Jesus as if he committed the believer's sins. The eternal wrath of God was poured out on the eternal Son of God on the cross. The righteousness of Jesus was transferred to the believer. In God's eyes, the believer is now washed, blameless, and holy only because of Jesus. It has absolutely nothing to do with service (good works), as righteousness is imputed (credited) to the believer.

Unbelievers—those who have not confessed to God that they are lost sinners and have not received Christ as Lord and Savior. All their sins remain with them, and the eternal wrath of God is upon those sins, therefore upon the sinner. They possess their own righteousness, which, when compared to Jesus' righteousness, is declared by God as unrighteousness—some are religious, and some are not but all are lost.

"^{2} For I bear them witness that they have a zeal for God, but not according to knowledge. ^{3} For they being ignorant of God's righteousness, and seeking to establish their own righteousness, have not submitted to the righteousness of God. ^{4} For Christ is the end of the law for righteousness to everyone who believes." **Romans 10:2-4**

They do not understand that the eternal God requires an eternal blood sacrifice to satisfy his eternal wrath upon sin. Only Jesus, the eternal Son of God, offered up by the eternal Holy Spirit, was able to accomplish that for all sinners.

"^{14} How much more, then, will the blood of Christ, who through the eternal Spirit offered himself unblemished to God, cleanse our consciences from acts that lead to death, so that we may serve the living God!" **Hebrews 9:14**

CHAPTER 2

The Enemy of God

One world, two groups. God is Father to believers and is Judge to unbelievers. All believers are called saints, while all unbelievers are called the wicked. God's interaction with each group is 180 degrees apart. From the Lord's perspective, the believers are under grace and are treated as children. Unbelievers are under wrath and are treated as enemies who are at war against God.

You may say: Now wait a minute, I am not an enemy of God, and I am definitely not at war with God!

Well, my friend, you may not be an enemy and at war with God, but God said that He is your enemy and is at war with you. He has also declared that you are currently and will forever be under the wrath of God if you remain an unbeliever.

"[36] Whoever believes in the Son has eternal life, but whoever rejects the Son will not see life, **for God's wrath abides on them.**" **John 3:36**

That word abides means that the wrath of God is currently on the unbeliever and will continue forever unless one believes during their lifetime on earth.

In **Col. 3:5-6,** Paul calls the unbelievers the children of disobedience and states, "⁵ Put to death, therefore, whatever belongs to your earthly nature: sexual immorality, impurity, lust, evil desires, and greed, which is idolatry. ⁶ For which things sake, the **wrath of God continues on the children of disobedience.**"

The word continues means forever, throughout all eternity. Most unbelievers are unaware of all the attributes of God. They are familiar with his love, gentleness, kindness, grace, and maybe even his immutability and omniscience but are keenly ignorant of his glory, holiness, and wrath. They promote ones they like and disregard his other attributes. Yet, God's wrath is equivalent to all his other attributes, although it is not his preference to display it. Nonetheless, the Lord must be true to himself by glorifying his holiness and displaying his wrath upon sin.

"¹⁸ For **the wrath of God is revealed** from heaven against all ungodliness and unrighteousness of men, who holds the truth in unrighteousness." **Rom. 1:18**

"³ And even if our gospel is veiled (hidden), it is veiled to those who are perishing. ⁴ The god of this age (Satan) **has blinded the minds of unbelievers,** so that they cannot see the light of the gospel that displays the glory of Christ, who is the image of God." **2 Cor. 4:3-4**

You may think: I will come to God whenever I am ready.

No, you will not. Look again at the verse above. The devil has blinded your mind and convinced you to believe that. People come to God when He calls. Please understand this, salvation is of the Lord. He is the author and finisher of saving faith. Jesus is the One who gives faith and the One who maintains faith. Believers do not maintain their own faith; Jesus does.

"⁵ But because of your stubbornness and your **unrepentant heart, you are storing up wrath against yourself** for the day of ⁶ God's wrath, when his righteous judgment will be revealed. God "will repay each person according to what they have done." ⁸…**for those who are self-seeking and who reject the truth and follow evil, there will be wrath and anger." Rom. 2:5-6, 8**

My friend, there is a day of reckoning coming! God's wrath grows daily with the daily sins committed by the unbeliever.

"¹¹ God judges (sustains) the righteous and, God is **angry with the wicked (unbelievers) every day." Psalms 7:11**

"⁶ Seeing it is a righteous thing with God to recompense tribulation to them that trouble you; ⁷ and to you who are troubled rest with us, when the Lord Jesus shall be revealed from heaven with his mighty angels, ⁸ **in flaming fire (**the holiness of God**) taking vengeance on them that do not know God and do not obey the gospel** of our Lord Jesus Christ. Who shall be **punished with everlasting destruction** from the presence of the Lord, and the glory of his power; when he shall come to be glorified in his saints (all believers) and to be admired in all of them that believe (because our testimony among you was believed) in that day." **II Thes. 1:6-8**

This text points out the unbeliever's true nature; they do not know God and do not obey God. Also, note that the unbeliever's punishment will last forever.

"¹⁰…he himself (the unbeliever) shall also drink of the wine of the wrath of God, which is poured out full strength into the cup of His (God's) indignation. **He (the unbeliever) shall be tormented with fire and brimstone** in the presence of the holy angels and in the presence of the Lamb (Jesus). ¹¹ And **the smoke of their torment ascends forever and ever; and they have no rest day or night**…" Rev. 14:10-11

"1 Then I saw a great white throne and Him (Jesus) who sat on it, from whose face the earth and the heaven fled away. And there was found no place for them. ¹² And I saw the dead (in trespasses and sins), small and great, standing before God (the Lord Jesus Christ), and books were opened. And another book was opened, which is the Book of Life. And the dead (unbelievers) were judged according to their works, by the things which were written in the books. ¹³ The sea gave up the dead who were in it, and Death and Hades delivered up the dead who were in them. And they were judged, each one according to his works. ¹⁴ Then Death and Hades were cast into the lake of fire. This is the second death. ¹⁵ **And anyone not found written in the Book of Life was cast into the lake of fire.**" Rev. 20:11-15

Unbelievers are not urged to get into the lake of fire, nor do they voluntarily offer to jump in. On the contrary, they are cast, thrown into the lake of fire burning with brimstone. According to the Bible, the word of God, there is no such thing as purgatory, soul sleep, or annihilation. All that ever lived will be raised from the dead to stand before the Son of God, the Lord Jesus Christ, on judgment day.

I can continue, but you get the point.

CHAPTER 3

Is There Really A Hell?

You may say: I thought Jesus (God) loves everyone?

Unfortunately, my friend, that is not a biblical statement. Remember, it is not what you or I think but what does the Bible, God's word, says.

"Well," you say, "the Jesus I know is too loving and kind to send someone to hell."

Then the Jesus you know is a figment of your imagination and not the Jesus described in the Bible. Do you know who in the Bible talked more about hell than almost all others combined? Jesus did. Here are just a few statements that Jesus made concerning hell.

"[12] But the children of the kingdom shall be cast out into outer darkness: there shall be weeping and gnashing of teeth." **Matthew 8:12**

"[42] And shall cast them into a furnace of fire: there shall be wailing and gnashing of teeth." **Matthew 13:42**

"[50] And shall cast them into the furnace of fire: there shall be wailing and gnashing of teeth." **Matthew 13:50**

"¹³ Then said the king to the servants, bind him hand and foot, and take him away, and cast him into outer darkness; there shall be weeping and gnashing of teeth." **Matthew 22:13**

"⁵¹ And shall cut him asunder and appoint him his portion with the hypocrites: there shall be weeping and gnashing of teeth." **Matthew 24:51**

"³⁰ And cast ye the unprofitable servant into outer darkness: there shall be weeping and gnashing of teeth." **Matthew 25:30**

"⁴¹ "Then He will also say to those on the left hand, Depart from Me, you cursed, into the everlasting fire prepared for the devil and his angels:" **Matthew 25:41**

²⁴ "Then he cried and said, 'Father Abraham, have mercy on me, and send Lazarus that he may dip the tip of his finger in water and cool my tongue; for I am tormented in this flame.'" **Luke 16:24**

"²⁸ There shall be weeping and gnashing of teeth, when ye shall see Abraham, and Isaac, and Jacob, and all the prophets, in the kingdom of God, and you yourselves thrust out." **Luke 13:28**

"⁴³ If your hand causes you to stumble, cut it off. It is better for you to enter life maimed than with two hands to go into hell, where the fire never goes out…⁴⁸ where "'the worms that eat them do not die, and the fire is not quenched.'" **Mark 9:43, 48**

"¹⁷ These are wells without water, clouds carried by a tempest, for whom is reserved the blackness of darkness forever." **2 Peter 2:17**

"⁹ Then a third angel followed them, saying with a loud voice, "If anyone worships the beast and his image, and receives his mark

on his forehead or on his hand, [10] he himself shall also drink of the wine of the wrath of God, which is poured out full strength into the cup of His indignation. He shall be tormented with fire and brimstone in the presence of the holy angels and in the presence of the Lamb. [11] And the smoke of their torment ascends forever and ever; and they have no rest day or night, who worship the beast and his image, and whoever receives the mark of his name."
Revelation 14:9-11

"[14] Then Death and Hades were thrown into the lake of fire. The lake of fire is the second death. [15] Anyone whose name was not found written in the book of life was thrown into the lake of fire."
Revelation 20:14-15

So, does the Bible state that hell is real? Absolutely! Let's review in list format the descriptions of hell given by Jesus from the verses above. Hell is:

1. a place of eternal torment
2. a place of outer darkness
3. where the blackness of darkness resides forever
4. a place of weeping
5. a place of gnashing of teeth
6. a place of everlasting fire
7. where people's conscience will eat at them like a worm
8. where one will remember their earthly past
9. where the senses of touch, feel, sight, et al., are active
10. where people will have a physical body, finger, tongue, hand, teeth, etc., that cannot die
11. where the fire is never quenched

12. a place of complete eternal separation from the life of God and heaven
13. a lake filled with fire and brimstone
14. where there is no rest from torment day or night forever and ever
15. a place created for the devil and his demonic angels
16. In hell, everyone is a believer in Jesus Christ, but it is too late.

There is no escaping the truth that hell is real. No amount of wishful thinking, acts of denial, or pretense of nonexistence will invalidate the truth that God says hell is a real place. Not only is it a real place, but the sole purpose for its creation was for God's enemies, the devil, and his fellow rebel angels. This means that the original plan of God did not include any of mankind being sentenced to hell.

You ask: Then why would Jesus say that people will be judged and sentenced to hell?

The Lord provides the answer to this question through the prophet Isaiah.

"*¹²* But they do not regard the work of the LORD, nor consider the operation of His hands. *¹³* Therefore my people have gone into captivity, because they have no knowledge; Their honorable men are famished, and their multitude dried up with thirst. *¹⁴* Therefore Sheol (Hell) has enlarged itself and opened its mouth beyond measure; Their glory and their multitude and their pomp, and he who is jubilant, shall descend into it. *¹⁵* People shall be brought down, each man shall be humbled, And the eyes of the lofty shall be humbled. [16] But the LORD of hosts shall be exalted in judgment, And God who is holy shall be hallowed in righteousness." **Isaiah 5:12-16**

The sole reason given in the word of God for men being sentenced to hell is because everyone born into this world is born a sinner by inheritance from the seed of their father and alienated from God. The penalty for being a sinner is death, both physical and spiritual. We established from the word of God that everyone is born a sinner because everyone can die. The only way to be forgiven of our sins is to have someone else who does not have sin, who is as holy as God is, and as eternal as God is, take sins penalty in our place. Jesus Christ, the Son of God, is sinless, as holy and eternal as God, and have voluntarily taken sins penalty by dying on the cross. God showed His acceptance of Jesus' sacrifice when He raised Jesus from the grave. This made it possible for all people that repent and believe in Jesus to have their sin debt eradicated and given Jesus's righteousness, thereby escaping the wrath of God upon their sin in hell forever.

You may ask: Are you saying that everyone is going to hell?

No, I did not say that; God did. Listen to what Jesus said concerning everyone who has ever lived.

"[13] "Enter by the narrow gate; for wide is the gate and broad is the way that leads to destruction, and there are many who go in by it. [14] Because narrow is the gate and straight (difficult) is the way which leads to life, and there are few who find it." **Matthew 7:13-14**

In this section of the book of Matthew, the Lord Jesus, who is God, gives a synopsis of the people on earth and their journey through this life. He stated in the above verses that there are:

1. two gates, wide and narrow
2. two ways, broad and straight
3. two destinations, destruction and life and
4. two groups of people, many and few.

Both gates, the narrow and the wide, are assumed to provide the two different entrances to God's kingdom. Most believe this way because, in this life, two ways are offered to people, as there are two kingdoms. There is the Lord's kingdom and the devil's kingdom, but the kingdom of God rules over all, as He is the sovereign creator and is greater than the summation of all He created.

The entrance to the narrow gate is by faith, only through Jesus Christ, constricted and precise. The narrow gate and difficult way represent true salvation in God's way that leads to life eternal. We call this heaven. However, the entrance to the wide gate includes all religions of the world that depends upon good works, righteous deeds, like love, kindness, gentleness, penance, giving of alms, and all the other self-righteous acts men's minds can conceive, with no single way. These are the religious and the non-religious who are deceived, but this wide way with many paths leads to hell, not heaven. As Peter proclaimed to the religious Jews of his day,

"[10] let it be known to you all, and to all the people of Israel, that by the name of Jesus Christ of Nazareth, whom you crucified, whom God raised from the dead, by Him this man stands here before you whole. [11] This is the stone which was rejected by you builders, which has become the chief cornerstone.' ¹² Nor is there salvation in any other, for there is no other name under heaven given among men by which we must be saved." **Acts 4:10-12**

Jesus repeatedly emphasized the difficulty of following Him, as this was evident when reading the book John chapter 6.

"⁶⁰ Therefore many of His disciples, when they heard this, said, "This is a hard saying; who can understand it?" ⁶¹ When Jesus knew in Himself that His disciples complained about this, He said to them, "Does this offend you? ⁶² What then if you should see the Son of Man ascend where He was before? ⁶³ It is the Spirit who gives life; the flesh profits nothing. The words that I speak to you are spirit, and they are life. ⁶⁴ But there are some of you who do not believe." For Jesus knew from the beginning who they were who did not believe, and who would betray Him. ⁶⁵ And He said, "Therefore I have said to you that no one can come to Me unless it has been granted to him by My Father." ⁶⁶ From that time many of His disciples went back and walked with Him no more. ⁶⁷ Then Jesus said to the twelve, "Do you also want to go away?" **John 6:60-67**

Our response should be like Simon Peter along with the other ten disciples and say:

"⁶⁸ ..."Lord, to whom shall we go? You have the words of eternal life. ⁶⁹ Also we have come to believe and know that You are the Christ, the Son of the living God." **John 6:68-69**

Salvation is by grace alone through faith alone but is not an easy road to navigate. Saving faith calls for knowledge of the truth, repentance, submission to Christ as Lord, Savior, and God, plus a willingness to obey His will and Word.

There is one God and only one way to this one God, the only begotten Son of God, Jesus Christ the Lord.

"³ For this is good and acceptable in the sight of God our Savior, ⁴ who desires all men to be saved and to come to the knowledge of the truth. ⁵ For there is one God and one Mediator between God and men, the Man Christ Jesus, ⁶ who gave Himself a ransom for all, to be testified in due time," **1 Timothy 2:3-6**

* * *

Providing further contrast on the lifestyles of these two groups, Jesus said:

"¹⁵ "Beware of false prophets, who come to you in sheep's clothing, but inwardly they are ravenous wolves. ¹⁶ You will know them by their fruits. Do men gather grapes from thornbushes or figs from thistles? ¹⁷ Even so, every good tree bears good fruit, but a bad tree bears bad fruit. ¹⁸ A good tree cannot bear bad fruit, nor can a bad tree bear good fruit. ¹⁹ Every tree that does not bear good fruit is cut down and thrown into the fire. ²⁰ Therefore by their fruits you will know them." **Matthew 7:15-20**

In the above verses, it is revealed that there are:

1. two kinds of trees that produce and
2. two kinds of fruit.

Jesus declares that the people of each group can be identified, for the most part, by their fruit, which we call our lifestyle.

You ask: What do you mean by lifestyle?

The Bible states that people on the narrow way and straight path seek to please God. They are heavenly-minded, and their behavior, though not perfect, reflects that choice. Meanwhile, the people on the wide way and broad path seek to please themselves. They are earthly-minded, and their behavior and pursuits are all about things they can acquire and consume while alive on the earth. They never consider God and are only interested in pleasing themselves. This does not mean that they are criminals or mean or snobbish or disrespectful. Nevertheless, hell will be full of nice religious people along with openly rebellious and wicked people.

Next, the Lord states that there will be a judgment day and there will be on that day, two groups standing before the throne of Jesus,

1. Those He knows
2. Those He does not know.

"[21] "Not everyone who says to Me, 'Lord, Lord,' shall enter the kingdom of heaven, but he who does the will of My Father in heaven. [22] Many will say to Me in that day, 'Lord, Lord, have we not prophesied in Your name, cast out demons in Your name, and done many wonders in Your name?' [23] And then I will declare to them, 'I never knew you; depart from Me, you who practice lawlessness!'" **Matthew 7:21-23**

Notice it is the many who are entering at the wide gate and broad way who are pleading their case before the Lord Jesus. Also, note that only the religious people from that group who seek to justify themselves to the Lord depending solely on the good works they have performed. Yet, they will hear the Lord say to them, "I never knew you; depart from Me, you who practice lawlessness!"

The barrenness of this type of faith demonstrates its real character of those who are earthly-minded and on the wide way. Their service was intended to please God without true faith for salvation in Christ first. The faith that says but does not do is really unbelief. Jesus was not suggesting that works are meritorious for salvation, but that true faith will not fail to produce the fruit of good works. This was precisely the point of James when he stated that faith without works cannot be called faith. "[26] Faith without works is dead" (**James 2:26**), and dead faith is worse than no faith at all. Faith must work; it must produce; it must be visible. Verbal faith is not enough, and mental faith is insufficient.

Ending his sermon on the Mount of Olives, Jesus makes a comparison between the results of saving faith and mental faith.

"[24] "Therefore whoever hears these sayings of Mine, and does them, I will liken him to a wise man who built his house on the rock: [25] and the rain descended, the floods came, and the winds blew and beat on that house; and it did not fall, for it was founded on the rock. [26] "But everyone who hears these sayings of Mine, and does not do them, will be like a foolish man who built his house on the sand: [27] and the rain descended, the floods came, and the winds blew and beat on that house; and it fell. And great was its fall." **Matthew 7:24-27**

The house represents a religious life, while the rain represents divine judgment. Only the one built on the foundation of obedience to God's Word stands, which calls for repentance, rejection of salvation by works, and trust in God's grace to save through

His merciful provision. The house that falls had its foundation built upon the earthly desires of the builder's heart, which in the end, will be consumed by fire. The consummation of all things will be when the Lord destroys this earth along with the current heaven and create a new heaven and new earth as declared by the apostle, Peter.

"[10] But the day of the Lord will come as a thief in the night, in which the heavens will pass away with a great noise, and the elements will melt with fervent heat; both the earth and the works that are in it will be burned up. [11] Therefore, since all these things will be dissolved, what manner of persons ought you to be in holy conduct and godliness, [12] looking for and hastening the coming of the day of God, because of which the heavens will be dissolved, being on fire, and the elements will melt with fervent heat? [13] Nevertheless we, according to His promise, look for new heavens and a new earth in which righteousness dwells." **2 Peter 3:10-13**

How useless in that day will be the treasures of the unbeliever? What good will their cars, houses, money, power, and prestige be? All that they lived for will go up in smoke.

CHAPTER 4

Who Is Jesus Christ?

What do you see in your mind's eye when the name of Jesus is mentioned? Mary holding her little baby? Jesus hanging on a cross on some figurine? A cute picture of some actor?

Let me show you how Jesus looked before becoming a man then what He looks like today after the cross and resurrection.

Before

"[1] **I saw the Lord, high and exalted, seated on a throne; and the train of his robe filled the temple...** [3] **Holy, holy, holy is the LORD Almighty**; the whole earth is full of his glory... [5] "Woe to me!" I cried. "I am ruined! For I am a man of unclean lips, and I live among a people of unclean lips, and my eyes have seen the King, the LORD Almighty." **Isaiah 6:1, 3, 5**

"[26] Above the vault over their heads was what looked like a throne of lapis lazuli, and high above on the throne was a figure like that of a man. [27] I saw that from what appeared to be **his waist up he looked like glowing metal, as if full of fire, and that from there down he looked like fire; and brilliant light surrounded him.** [28] **Like the appearance of a rainbow in the clouds on a rainy day, so was the radiance around him.** This was the appearance of the likeness of the glory of the LORD. When I saw it, I fell facedown" **Ezekiel 1:26-28**

⁵ I looked up and there before me was a **man dressed in linen, with a belt of fine gold from Uphaz around his waist.** ⁶ **His body was like topaz, his face like lightning, his eyes like flaming torches, his arms and legs like the gleam of burnished bronze, and his voice like the sound of a multitude.** ⁷ I, Daniel, was the only one who saw the vision; those who were with me did not see it, but such terror overwhelmed them that they fled and hid themselves. ⁸ So, I was left alone, gazing at this great vision; I had no strength left, my face turned deathly pale, and I was helpless. ⁹ Then I heard him speaking, and as I listened to him, I fell into a deep sleep, my face to the ground. **Daniel 10:5-9**

Today

⁸ **I am the Alpha and the Omega," says the Lord God, "who is, and who was, and who is to come, the Almighty.** ¹² I (John) turned around to see the voice that was speaking to me. And when I turned, I saw seven golden lampstands, ¹³ and among the lampstands was someone **like a son of man, dressed in a robe reaching down to his feet and with a golden sash around his chest.** ¹⁴ **The hair on his head was white like wool, as white as snow, and his eyes were like blazing fire.** ¹⁵ **His feet were like bronze glowing in a furnace, and his voice was like the sound of rushing waters.** ¹⁶ In his right hand he held seven stars, and coming out of his mouth was a sharp, double-edged sword (His words). His face was like the sun shining in all its brilliance. ¹⁷ When I saw him, I fell at his feet as though dead. **Revelation 1:8, 12-17**

¹¹ I saw heaven standing open and there before me was a white horse, whose rider is called **Faithful and True. With justice he judges and wages war.** ¹² **His eyes are like blazing fire, and on his head are many crowns.** He has a name written on him that no one knows but he himself. ¹³ He is dressed in a robe dipped in blood, **and his name is the Word of God.** ¹⁴ The armies of heaven were following him, riding on white horses and dressed in fine linen, white and clean. ¹⁵ Coming out of his mouth is a sharp sword with which to strike down the nations. "He will rule them with an iron scepter." **He treads the winepress of the fury of the wrath of God Almighty.** ¹⁶ On his robe and on his thigh, he has this name written: **KING OF KINGS AND LORD OF LORDS. Revelation 19:11-16**

"¹¹ Then I saw a **great white throne and Jesus** was seated on it. The **earth and the heavens fled from his presence**, and there was no place for them. in the books. **Revelation 20:11**

"¹⁴…until the appearing of our Lord Jesus Christ, ¹⁵ which God will bring about in his own time —God, the blessed and only Ruler, the King of kings and Lord of lords, ¹⁶ **who alone is immortal and who lives in unapproachable light**, whom no one has seen or can see. To him be honor and might forever. Amen." **1 Timothy 6:14-16**

That is what Jesus looks like today. He is high, lifted up, exalted above all creation, majestic in holiness, radiant in glory, fearful in praises, working wonders. Everyone who sees Him will fall upon their face at His feet. He alone is God!

PART 2

IN CHRIST ALONE BY FAITH ALONE

CHAPTER 1

Jesus Is God The Savior

Members of the body of believers in Christ's redemptive work on the cross, His death, burial, and resurrection, were selected by God himself to reveal His attributes of mercy and grace throughout the ages to come.

"⁴ But because of his great love for us, God, who is rich in mercy, ⁵ **made us alive with Christ** even when we were dead in transgressions, it is by grace you have been saved. ⁶ And God raised us up with Christ and seated us with him in the heavenly realms in Christ Jesus (why did you do this Lord?), ⁷ **in order that in the coming ages (1,000 years earthly reign of Jesus and eternity) he might show the incomparable riches of his grace, expressed in his kindness to us in Christ Jesus.** Ephesians 2:4-7

"³ Blessed be the God and Father of our Lord Jesus Christ, who hath blessed us with all spiritual blessings in heavenly places in Christ: ⁴ According as **he hath chosen us in him before the foundation of the world,** that we **should be holy and without blame** before him in love. ⁵ Having **predestinated us** unto the adoption of children **by Jesus Christ** to himself **according to the good pleasure of his will, to** ⁶ **the**

praise of the glory of his grace, wherein he hath **made us accepted in the beloved.** ⁷ In whom we have **redemption through his blood,** the forgiveness of sins, **according to the riches of his grace**; wherein he hath abounded toward us **in all wisdom and prudence," Eph. 1:3-8**

The Lord God purposed this of his own volition without any outside influence.

You may ask: How do you know that? Well, verse 4 states that this decision to redeem a remnant from among the inhabitants of the earth was made by God "before the foundation of the world." The question then becomes, were you and I around before the foundation of the world to perform good deeds that prompted God to select us? The obvious answer to that rhetorical question is: No, we were not. This is the Spirit of God's response to such thinking; we read in verses 9 through 12.

"⁹Having made known unto us **the mystery of his will,** according to **his good pleasure** which he hath **purposed in himself**: ¹⁰ that in the dispensation of the fulness of times **he might gather** together in one **all things in Christ,** both which are in heaven, and which are on earth, even in him: ¹¹ in whom also we have **obtained an inheritance, being predestinated** according to the purpose of him who worketh all things after the counsel of his own will: ¹² that we should be **to the praise of his glory,** who first **trusted in Christ." Eph. 1:9-12**

"³⁷All those **the Father gives me will come to me,** and whoever comes to me I will never drive away." **John 6:37**

"⁴⁴**No one can come to me unless the Father who sent me draws them,** and I will raise them up at the last day." **John 6:44**

"²⁷My sheep listen to my voice; I know them, and they follow me. ²⁸ I give them eternal life, and they shall never perish; no one will snatch them out of my hand. ²⁹ **My Father, who has given them to me**, is greater than all; no one can snatch them out of my Father's hand. ³⁰ I and the Father are one." **John 10:27-30**

What's the point that the Father is making here? That no person, in and of themselves, has the ability to determine whether they will believe in Christ. The call of the Father is the gospel. All who hear the gospel and respond in faith at the prompting of the Holy Spirit are the **called ones** who are regenerated and given as a love gift by the Father to the Son.

The common mistake made by most is that we totally underestimate the inherent depravity of man's heart. **Jeremiah 17:9** states, "The heart is deceitful above all things, and desperately wicked: who can know it?" That word deceitful means insidiously polluted. The Lord is saying through Jeremiah the prophet that the fallen wicked nature of the spirit of man in a gradual, subtle way, but with extremely harmful intent and effects, infiltrates the thoughts and behavior of the individual, with the sole purpose of contaminating the entirety of a person's being with poisonous incurable immorality.

The question then becomes: If God has chosen a remnant to believe unto salvation, did God also choose everyone else to be condemned to hell? The short answer is no. God has provided a Savior for all people. Jesus is the lamb of God that takes away the sins of the world, not just the elect, called, or chosen. One of the most popular versus in the Bible proclaims:

"¹⁶God so loved the world that he gave his only begotten Son, that **whosoever believeth in him** should not perish, but have everlasting life." **John 3:16**

"⁴Who will have **all men** to be saved, and to come unto the knowledge of the truth." **1 Tim. 2:4**

"¹⁷For God sent not his Son into the world to condemn the world; but **that the world** through him might be saved." **John 3:17**

"²¹And it shall come to pass, that **whosoever shall call** on the name of the Lord shall be saved." **Acts 2:21**

"¹³For **whosoever shall call** upon the name of the Lord shall be saved." **Rom. 10:13**

"⁹The Lord is not slack concerning his promise, as some men count slackness; but is longsuffering toward us, **not willing that any should perish, but that all should come to repentance.**" **2 Pet. 3:9**

"¹⁴ And the grace of our Lord was exceedingly abundant, with faith and love which are in Christ Jesus. ¹⁵ This is a faithful saying and worthy of all acceptance, that Christ Jesus came into the world to save sinners, of whom I am chief." **1 Timothy 1:14-15**

"⁴⁵ For even the Son of Man did not come to be served, but to serve, and to give His life a ransom for many." **Mark 10:45**

"¹¹ For the Son of Man has come to save that which was lost." **Matthew 18:11**

The scriptures state that salvation is for all who believe in the Son of God. What is it that must be believed? We were all born sinners, unrighteous, deceitful liars, enemies of God condemned to hell, and that God is holy, righteous, just, and true. As sinners, we are separated from God, dead in trespasses and sins, and deserve to be punished for our sins, with the penalty being death. God of his own volition sent his Son, Jesus, into the world to take our punishment for sins. God punished Jesus as if He committed my sin and your sin. God accepted Jesus' death on the cross as payment for our sins, with the proof being the resurrection of Christ bodily from the grave. God accepts our belief in Jesus' death, burial, and resurrection and gives us Jesus' righteousness and eternal life.

God is eternal. His holiness is eternal. His wrath upon sin is eternal. **Jesus is that eternal God** who came down from heaven and inserted Himself into the body of a man. It is said of Jesus:

"[2]Before the mountains were born or you (Jesus) brought forth the whole world, from **everlasting to everlasting you (Jesus) are God**." **Psalms 90:2**

Jesus is eternally holy. It is said of Jesus, "[26]…**who is holy**, blameless, pure, set apart from sinners, exalted above the heavens." **Hebrews 7:26**

Because Jesus is eternal and eternally holy, He alone can bear the eternal wrath of the holy God.

CHAPTER 2

Condemned? Why God?

So, if God is love, who provided a Savior for all men, and wants all men to be saved, why then, will most be lost and condemned to hell? How is that fair?

First, we need to understand the most powerful attribute of the one true God. The LORD GOD is holy!

"³Let them praise thy great and terrible name; **for it is holy.**" **Psalms 99:3**

"⁹Exalt the LORD our God, and worship at his holy hill; **for the LORD, our God is holy.**" **Ps. 99:9**

"⁹**Holy and reverend is his name**. The fear of the LORD is the beginning of wisdom: ¹⁰a good understanding have all they that do his commandments: his praise endures forever" **Ps. 111:9-10**

The LORD GOD is so holy that he had to veil (humble) himself just to create the heavens and the earth because nothing he creates can withstand the full brightness of his majestic glory.

"⁴The LORD is high above all nations, and his glory above the heavens. ⁵Who is like unto the LORD our God, who dwells on high, "**who humbles himself to behold the things that are in heaven, and in the earth!" Ps. 113:4-6**

"³And one cried unto another, and said, **Holy, holy, holy, is the LORD of hosts,** the whole earth is full of his glory." **Isaiah 6:3**

"⁸The four living creatures, each having six wings, were full of eyes around and within. And they do not rest day or night, saying, "**Holy, holy, holy, Lord God Almighty**, Who was and is and is to come!" **Rev. 4:8**

Second, we need to be absolutely clear, God is righteous and just. It is impossible for him to be unjust. Just is who God is and not what he does. We see fairness or justice through the eyes of an evil perverted heart; therefore, our sense of justice, fairness, right, and wrong are warped and corrupt.

"¹⁷**The LORD is righteous in all his ways,** and holy in all his works." **Ps 145:17**

"¹³ Let all creation rejoice before the LORD, for he comes, he comes to judge the earth. **He will judge the world in righteousness and the peoples in his faithfulness" Psalms 96:13**

"⁷**The works of his hands are faithful and just**; all his precepts are trustworthy. ⁸ They are established for ever and ever, enacted in faithfulness and uprightness." **Psalms 111:7-8**

Third, every person born to man is born a sinner and deserves to be condemned to hell. Everyone! That is the justice we all deserve. The penalty for being a sinner is death.

I want you to think of a person you believe to be the most outstanding, upright, moral person who ever lived. Let us exclude

Jesus from this exercise. Do you have someone in mind? Okay, this is what the Bible says about that person:

"⁵Surely, I was sinful **at birth, sinful from the time my mother conceived me.**" **Ps. 51:5**

"¹As for you, you were **dead in your transgressions and sins**, in which you used to live when you followed the ways of this world and of the ruler of the kingdom of the air, **the spirit who is now at work in those who are disobedient**. ²All of us also lived among them at one time, gratifying the cravings of our flesh and following its desires and thoughts. ³Like the rest, **we were by nature deserving of wrath**." **Eph. 2:1-3**

"¹³And you, **being dead in your sins**" **Col. 2:13**

"¹⁰As it is written: ¹¹ "There is **no one righteous, not even one**; there is no one who understands; there is **no one who seeks God**. ¹² All have turned away, they have all together become **worthless; there is no one who does good, not even one**." ¹³ "Their throats are open graves, their tongues practice deceit." "The poison of vipers is on their lips." ¹⁴ "Their mouths are full of cursing and bitterness." ¹⁵ "Their feet are swift to shed blood; ¹⁶ ruin and misery mark their ways, ¹⁷ and the way of peace they do not know. ¹⁸ There is no fear of God before their eyes." **Rom. 3:10-18**

My friend, God's starting position is pure holiness and righteousness. Our starting position is condemned sinners. Is it possible for a filthy sinner to produce righteousness?

Listen to **Job 14:4** "Who can bring a clean thing out of an unclean? **Not one.**"

Job 15:14-15, "What is man, that he should be clean? And he which is born of a woman, that he should be righteous? Behold, he puts no trust in his saints, yea, **the heavens are not clean in his (God's) sight**."

Beloved our God is holy. Then Job asked the right question, **Job 25:4-6** "How then can man be righteous before God? Or how can he be pure who is born of a woman? If even **the moon does not shine, and the stars are not pure in His sight**, how much less man, who is a maggot, and a son of man, who is a worm?"

You may ask: How did we become sinners at birth?

Well, we were sold.

Sold? Sold by whom?

By Adam, the first man God created.

To whom did Adam sell us?

He sold us to the devil, who is also known as Satan.

Rom. 5:12 and 18 "Wherefore, as by one man (Adam) sin entered into the world, and death by sin; and so death passed upon all men, for that all have sinned...Therefore as by the offence of one (man, Adam) **judgement came upon all men to condemnation**..."

Now, do not get the ludicrous idea that God and Satan are equals. Infinitely far from it. Satan is an angel, created like all the other angels, by God. God is greater than the summation of all He has created. There is none like the Lord in the heavens above or the earth beneath or under the earth, visible or invisible. The Lord

God rule is sovereign, and none can stay his hand or say unto him: What are you doing?

"¹² You (Satan), were the seal of perfection, Full of wisdom and perfect in beauty. ¹³ You were in Eden, the garden of God; Every precious stone was your covering: The sardius, topaz, and diamond, Beryl, onyx, and jasper, Sapphire, turquoise, and emerald with gold. The workmanship of your timbrels and pipes was prepared for you on the day you (Satan) were created. ¹⁴ "You were the anointed cherub highest order of angels who covers; I God established you; You were on the holy mountain of God; You walked back and forth in the midst of fiery stones. ¹⁵ You were perfect in your ways from the day you were created, till iniquity was found in you. ¹⁶ "By the abundance of your trading you became filled with violence within, and you sinned; Therefore, I cast you as a profane thing out of the mountain of God; and I destroyed you, O covering cherub, from the midst of the fiery stones." **Ezekiel 28:12-16**

Do you want proof that you were born a sinner? Can you die? Only sinners die. The only reason anyone dies is because that is sin's penalty.

"²³ **For the wages of sin is death**; but the gift of God is eternal life through Jesus Christ our Lord" **Rom. 6:23**

In Romans 7:14, Paul said, "For we know that the law (Mosaic Law) is spiritual: but I am carnal, **sold under sin**."

You ask: Well, who sold Paul under sin?

Adam did.

To whom did he sell us?

Like I said before, to Satan.

You may say: Well, wait just one cotton-picking minute, Kevin. Are you saying that I am a child of the devil?

No, I did not say that; God did.

Listen to **Luke 4:5-6**, speaking of Jesus' temptations, "**and the devil,** taking him up into a high mountain, shewed unto him (Jesus) all the kingdoms of the world in a moment of time. And the devil said unto him (Jesus), All this power **will I (the devil) give** thee, and the glory of them: **for that is delivered unto me (the devil)**; and to whomsoever I will I give it."

The devil says that the kingdoms of this world were "delivered unto" him and Jesus, who is God, did not correct him. Who delivered the kingdoms of this world to him? Adam did. I am sorry to inform you that we are all born into the devil's family.

The apostle Paul told Timothy in **2 Tim. 2:24-26** "And the servant of the Lord must not strive; but be gentle unto all men, ready to teach, patient, in meekness instructing those that oppose themselves; if God peradventure will give them repentance to the acknowledging of the truth; and **that they (all men) may recover themselves out of the snare (slave pit) of the devil, who are taken captive by him at his will.**"

You and I were born into the devil's family. The only way of escape is to be born into the family of God through faith in Jesus Christ. No one can join the family of God. You must be born again. There is an old saying that goes, born once die twice; born twice die once.

"¹² Yet to all who did receive him (Jesus by faith), to those who believed in his name, he (Jesus) gave the right to become children of God, ¹³**children born not of natural descent, nor of human decision** or **the human will, but born of God." John 1:12-13**.

Jesus told a Jewish priest, Nicodemus, that he must be born again. Nicodemus was born into the right earthly family (natural descent). Nicodemus joined a religion (human decision). Nicodemus did good deeds and religious works (human will). Yet, none of those things could ever take him from being a child of Satan to a child of God, nor could it eradicate his sins.

Therefore, if God gave us all justice, we would all be sent to hell. That is what we deserve because we are all sinners. Hence, if God, in His righteous judgment, finds us guilty and sentences us to hell, we deserve it—all of us! That is justice and fairness from the God of love, who is also a holy God that cannot compromise with or look upon sin.

Listen to God, "²All the ways of a man are clean in his own eyes; but the Lord weighs the spirits (the real you that lives inside your body)." **Prov. 16:2**

In Prov. **14:12,** God says, "¹²There is a way that seems right unto a man, but the end thereof are the ways of death."

The Lord God, speaking with the prophet Haggai concerning religious practices of the children of Israel, **Hag. 2:13-14** "¹³Then said Haggai, if one that is unclean by a dead body (that's us, dead in trespasses and sins) touch any of these (holy things of God), shall it be unclean? ¹⁴And the priests answered and said, it shall be unclean."

Here is the question: Can an unbelieving unsaved, unregenerate unclean wretched, wicked, deceitful sinner offer up worship and praise to a holy God? The answer is, absolutely not!

This is what God thinks about religious people; **v. 14** "Then answered Haggai, and said, so is this people, and so is this nation before me, saith the Lord; and so is every work of their hands; and **that which they offer there is unclean**."

Friend, you cannot come to God in your filthy condition and offer up worship and praise to him. The unbeliever's worship and praise are unholy and unclean; therefore, it is a sin. He will not accept it. You must be made holy first by the blood of Jesus and the regeneration (new birth) of the Holy Spirit.

You may say: "But I am sincere in my worship and service to God."

That does not matter! The Lord God, the Holy One of Israel, has determined how man may enter into his presence. He cannot compromise with sin. He is holy!

Listen to the Most High God:

"[16]But to the wicked person (the unbeliever), God says: "What right have you to recite my laws or take my covenant on your lips? [17] You hate my instruction and cast my words behind you. [18] When you see a thief, you join with him; you throw in your lot with adulterers. [19] You use your mouth for evil and harness your tongue to deceit. [20] You sit and testify against your brother and slander your own mother's son. [21] When you did these things and I kept silent, you thought I was exactly like you. But I now charge you and set my accusations before you." **Ps. 50:16-21**

* * *

Now, let's go back to the book of **John chapter 3** to everyone's favorite **verse, 16**; for God so loved the world and continue to read through **verse 18**.

"¹⁶For God so loved the world that He gave His only begotten Son, that whoever believes in Him should not perish but have everlasting life. ¹⁷ For God did not send His Son into the world to condemn the world, but that the world through Him might be saved. ¹⁸ "He who believes in Him is not condemned; but he who does not believe is condemned already, because he has not believed in the name of the only begotten Son of God." **John 3:16-18**

V**erse 17** states that Jesus was sent into the world for the sole purpose of being a Savior. V**erse 18** states that if anyone believes in Jesus, that person is no longer condemned, but those who do not believe remain in the condemned state.

You may ask: Why?

Because they did not do the one thing God said was necessary for him to remove the condemnation, which is believe in Jesus. We are already condemned. That is the starting position we are born into. What does a person have to do to be condemned to hell? The answer is simply to be born. That's it, my friend. Being a "good" or religious person will not change that fact or transfer you out of the devil's family.

The better question is: Why wouldn't a person believe in Jesus?

Well, keep reading. V**erse 19** states, "and this is the condemnation, that light (Jesus) is come into the world, and **men (mankind) loved darkness** (our hearts) **rather than light** (God is light), (WHY?) **because their deeds were evil.**"

This is the problem with everyone who remains lost, in unbelief, and is condemned to hell. **Verse 20** sums it up; "For everyone that does evil hates the light, neither comes to the light, unless his deeds should be reproved"

Jesus told the religious Jews, [40] "you will not come to me, that you might be saved.**" John 5:40**

"[41] I said therefore unto you, that you shall die in your sins: for **if you believe not** that I am he (the Messiah, Savior of the world), you shall die in your sins." **John 8:24**

Paul said that people will be deceived, [10] "because they **received not the love of the truth**, that they might be saved." **2 Thes. 2:10**

Paul expounded upon this truth in Romans. [18] "The wrath of God is being revealed from heaven against all the godlessness and wickedness of unbelievers, who suppress the truth by their wicked behavior" **Rom. 1:18**

Verse 21 states, "because that, when they knew God, they glorified him not as God, neither were thankful; but became vain in their imaginations, and their foolish heart was darkened."

Now look at **verse 28**; "Furthermore, just as they did not think it worthwhile to retain the knowledge of God, so God gave them over to a depraved mind, so that they do what ought not to be done."

Finally, in **verse 32**, "Although they know God's righteous judgement that those who do such things deserve death, **they not only continue to do these very things but also approve of those who practice them.**"

So, why don't people believe in Jesus?

- They love darkness.
- They hate the light.
- Their deeds are evil.
- They refuse to come to Jesus.
- They don't want anyone to tell them to stop sinning.
- They reject the offer of salvation.
- They hate the truth (God's word).
- They hold the truth in unrighteousness (they suppress the truth by calling good—evil and evil—good).
- They refuse to acknowledge God's sovereignty.
- They are unthankful.
- They follow their own way.
- They pursue unrighteousness.
- They refuse to think about God.
- They do things that are against nature.
- They mock the pending judgment of God.
- They openly and boastfully rebel against God.
- They encourage others to do the same.
- They elect those who are like them to power.

This is why people will go to hell. God did not predestine anyone to hell. On the contrary, through his love, he provided a Savior. Unfortunately, God does not save anyone through love. Salvation is only offered by grace through faith.

"¹ As for you, you were dead in your transgressions and sins, ² in which you used to live when you followed the ways of this world and of the ruler of the kingdom of the air, the spirit who is now at work in those who are disobedient. ³ All of us also lived among them at one time, gratifying the cravings of our flesh and following its desires and thoughts. Like the rest, we were by nature deserving of wrath. ⁴ But because of his great love for us, God, who is rich in mercy, ⁵ made us alive with Christ even when we were dead in transgressions, **it is by grace you have been saved**. ⁶ And God raised us up with Christ and seated us with him in the heavenly realms in Christ Jesus, ⁷ in order that in the coming ages he might show the incomparable riches of his grace, expressed in his kindness to us in Christ Jesus. ⁸ **For it is by grace you have been saved, through faith and this is not from yourselves, it is the gift of God ⁹ not by works, so that no one can boast.** ¹⁰ For we are God's handiwork, created in Christ Jesus to do good works, which God prepared in advance for us to do. **Ephesians 2:1-10**

People's utter refusal of God's free gift, salvation through faith in Jesus Christ, and their relentless pursuit of earthly possessions and evil deeds, are what send them to a God-less eternity in hell. They get exactly what they seek, a world without a holy God and judgment based on their behavior (good works). The verdict at that trial will always be guilty as charged. They will all hear God say, depart from me, you who does lawless acts, into the everlasting fire prepared for the devil and his angels.

You can change your destiny, here and now. Remember, you are already a condemned child of the devil, and as we have proven, in the eyes of God, there is no such thing as a "good person." You can believe the record that God gave of his Son, Jesus Christ, and by faith be translated from the kingdom of darkness to the kingdom of light. Jesus said, him that comes to me, I will in no wise cast out.

Remember, no prayer can save you, as there is no salvation in the sincerity of words. You are not too bad that you cannot be saved. You are not too good that you do not need to be saved. No amount of church attendance can save you. No amount of good or religious deeds can save you. Only Jesus can save you, through faith in His death, burial, and resurrection.

"[8] But what does God say? His words are near you; it is in your mouth and in your heart, that is, the message concerning faith that we proclaim: [9] If you declare with your mouth, "Jesus is Lord," and believe in your heart that God raised him from the dead, you will be saved. [10] For it is with your heart that you believe and are justified, and it is with your mouth that you profess your faith and are saved. **Romans 10:8-10**

If you have read this, the voice of God by his words and through his Holy Spirit is calling you right now, saying:

"[7] ..."Today, if you hear his voice, [8] do not harden your hearts." **Hebrews 3:7-8**

What say you? Will you answer the call of God right now and be saved?

CHAPTER 3

There Is Hope In Jesus and The Evidence of Saving Faith

What must I do to be saved?

Confess to God that you are a sinner and cannot save yourself. Repent of your rebellion against the holy God. Confess that you believe that He (God) punished Jesus as if Jesus committed all your sins, past, present, and future. Believe that Jesus alone can save you by crying out and asking Him to forgive your sins and save you. Be willing to turn from your sinful ways and begin to study and obey the word of God. Ask Jesus to save you.

If you truly meant business with God from your heart, then the evidence of salvation will be present in your life.

You ask: What is that evidence?

You will love God the Father and Jesus more than you love yourself. You will love what God the Father and Jesus love, righteousness, God's people in Israel (the Jews) and his children (other believers).

[15] "If you love me, keep my commandments...[21] Whoever has my commandments and keeps them is the one who loves me. The

one who loves me will be loved by my Father, and I too will love them and show myself to them." **John 14:15, 21**

Followed by an unquenchable desire for the word of God, an overwhelming desire to obey the word of God, immediate conviction of disobedience against the word of God, and peaceful fruits (works) of righteousness produced by the Spirit of God living inside of you. No, not for salvation but evidence that your salvation is real.

"[17] Therefore, if anyone is in Christ, he is a new creation; old things have passed away; behold, all things have become new." **2 Corinthians 5:17**

True faith in Christ produces righteous works. Now listen, and this is extremely important.

If you find yourself living in your past sinful ways without conviction by conscience, correction by the Holy Spirit, and chastisement by the Lord, all of which leads the believer back to obedience to the word of God, then you can be assured that you have never possessed saving faith and are still in your sins and on your way to hell. Saving biblical faith is evidenced through believers' willful surrendering of their lives (wants and desires) to become slaves of Christ because we love Him who first loved us and gave his life for our salvation.

Paul told the believers in the church at Corinth to "[5] Examine yourselves to see whether you are in the faith; test yourselves. Do you not realize that Christ Jesus is in you unless, of course, you fail the test?" **2 Corinthians 13:5**

Why would Paul tell "believers" to examine themselves?

"²⁰ For I am afraid that when I come, I may not find you as I want you to be, and you may not find me as you want me to be. I fear that there may be discord, jealousy, fits of rage, selfish ambition, slander, gossip, arrogance, and disorder. Embolden all of verse²¹. I am afraid that when I come again my God will humble me before you, and I will be grieved over many who have sinned earlier and have not repented of the impurity, sexual sin, and debauchery in which they have indulged." **2 Corinthians 12:20-21**

Because the evidence of saving faith was not being demonstrated in their lives.

"⁶ For in Christ Jesus neither circumcision (participation in religious rituals) nor uncircumcision (non-participation in religious rituals) has any value. The only thing that counts is faith expressing itself through love." **Galatians 5:6**

How does saving faith express itself through love? It is revealed to the world through our uncompromising obedience to the word of God.

"³² We are witnesses of these things, and so is the Holy Spirit, **whom God has given to those who obey him." Acts 5:32**

"¹⁵What then? Shall we (believers) sin because we are not under the law but under grace? **By no means!** ¹⁶ Don't you know that when you offer yourselves to someone as obedient slaves, you are slaves of the one you obey—whether you are slaves to sin, which leads to death, or **to obedience, which leads to righteousness**? ¹⁷ But thanks be to God that, though you used to be slaves to sin, **you have come to obey from your heart** the pattern of teaching that has now claimed your allegiance. ¹⁸ You have been set free from sin and **have become slaves to righteousness." Romans 6:15-18**

Beloved do not be deceived. God only gives the Holy Spirit and salvation to those who lovingly and willingly obey Him. Believers are commanded to be as obedient to Christ as Christ is obedient to the Father. The Father loves the Son because the Son is willingly and perfectly obedient and only has one goal, to do the Father's will. That is the relationship that we have with Christ. We are slaves by choice, denying ourselves, living every second of our lives in service to our Master, who is also our Friend.

How does Christ obey the Father? I will let Jesus tell you.

"[29] And He who sent Me is with Me. The Father has not left Me alone, for I always do those things that please Him." **John 8:29**

"[9] He (Jesus) became the source of eternal salvation for **all who obey him**" **Hebrews 5:9**

"[5] Through Him we have received grace and apostleship **for obedience to the faith** among all nations for His name, [6] among whom you also are the called of Jesus Christ;" **Romans 1:5-6**

"[2] elect according to the foreknowledge of God the Father, in sanctification of the Spirit, **for obedience** and sprinkling of the blood of Jesus Christ:" **1 Peter 1:2**

"[16] Do you not know that to whom you present yourselves slaves to obey, you are that one's slaves whom you obey, whether of sin leading to death, or of obedience leading to righteousness? [17] But God be thanked that though you were slaves of sin, **yet you obeyed from the heart that form of doctrine** to which you were delivered." **Romans 6:16-17**

Will you move from being an unbeliever to a believer today?

From the kingdom of Satan to the Kingdom of Christ?

God is calling you now. Repent and believe the gospel of Jesus Christ, the Son of the Most High God. Jesus will save to the utmost those that come to him in faith. Do not delay any longer, my friend. Call upon Jesus today and get on the narrow way and straight path. You will find that Jesus is a loving, kind, merciful, and wonderful Savior.

THE END.

Notes

All scripture references are from:

New King James Version (KJV)
Publisher: Thomas Nelson
Copyright: All rights reserved
Build date: Tuesday, March 5, 2019

And

New International Version (NIV)
Publisher: Biblica
Copyright: © 1973, 1978, 1984, 2011 by Biblica, Inc.
Build date: Wednesday, October 23, 2019
Use of scripture falls within publishers' stated guidelines.

About The Author

Kevin Madison is an author, husband, and father who has walked faithfully with the Lord for over 28 years. The son of the late Pastor Leroy Phillips and Billie Mae Phillips who raised their 13 children to love and fear the God of salvation and King of righteousness.

Modeling his study pattern after his former Pastor, Carl Brown of Baton Rouge, LA and current favorite Pastors Dr. John Barnett and John MacArthur, Kevin has become proficient at dissecting the scriptures verse by verse. Greatly impacted by his affection and love for the late Dr. J. Vernon McGee who always challenged his listeners to study the entire word of God, Kevin has written many topical articles and yet to be published verse by verse Commentaries on the Old Testament Prophets. He is the author of several books including *Predestined to Hell? - Why Would a God Love Consign People to Hell FOREVER?*, *The Chastisement of the Lord – How Does God Respond When Christians Sin*, and *America - the Judgement of Sodom and Gomorrah*. With several other upcoming titles soon to be published including the much-anticipated title *Story of the Ages - God's Plan to Eliminate the Possibility of Sin*.

Kevin's love for the Lord has given him a passion to see the unbeliever converted into a believer, as he walks with Jesus daily while He seeks and save those that are lost. It is this compassion that prompted the writing of his book *Predestined to Hell? Why Would a God of Love Consign People to Hell FOREVER?* After walking with the Lord for over 28 years, personally experiencing the ebbs and flow of living in a world contaminated by the sins of others and that of his own, Kevin understands the need for prayer, Bible study, Christian fellowship, and encouragement. These principal life events led to the writing of his book titled *The Chastisement of the Lord – How Does God Respond When Christians Sin.*

Kevin also loves the calling card of God, prophesy. No one knows the future, nor can anyone predict future events with 100% accuracy but God. Therefore, he has devoted much study time to understanding the plan of God for heaven, hell, earth, angels, and people. The prophetic scriptures taken realistically and wholistically layouts in detail the ultimate plan of God while answering the key why question that all people have. Why, God, did you allow sin for the possibility of sin within your creation? Like most Christians, Kevin have been asked this question numerous times which have led to an exhaustive study to address it directly from God's word. This is the theme in Kevin's upcoming book titled Story of the Ages – God's Plan to Eliminate the Possibility of Sin.

It is with great joy, compassion, and truth of the word of God that Kevin has answered the call of the Lord with thanksgiving to write in book format the topics that God has placed on his heart. All to the edification of the church, salvation of the lost, and all honor, glory, and praise unto the Most High God and our Savior, the Lord Jesus Christ.

www.ingramcontent.com/pod-product-compliance
Lightning Source LLC
Chambersburg PA
CBHW020915080526
44589CB00011B/602